For my dear Carly

I love you so much! And Jesus loves you even more.

Mom

Then Jesus called for the children and said to the disciples,
"Let the children come to me. Don't stop them!
For the Kingdom of God belongs to those who are like these children.
I tell you the truth, anyone who doesn't receive the Kingdom of God like a child will never enter it."
— Luke 18:16-17

Hello Jesus, let's talk.

I am so glad you are right here with me.
I can talk with you in many different ways.
You talk to me in lots of ways too.

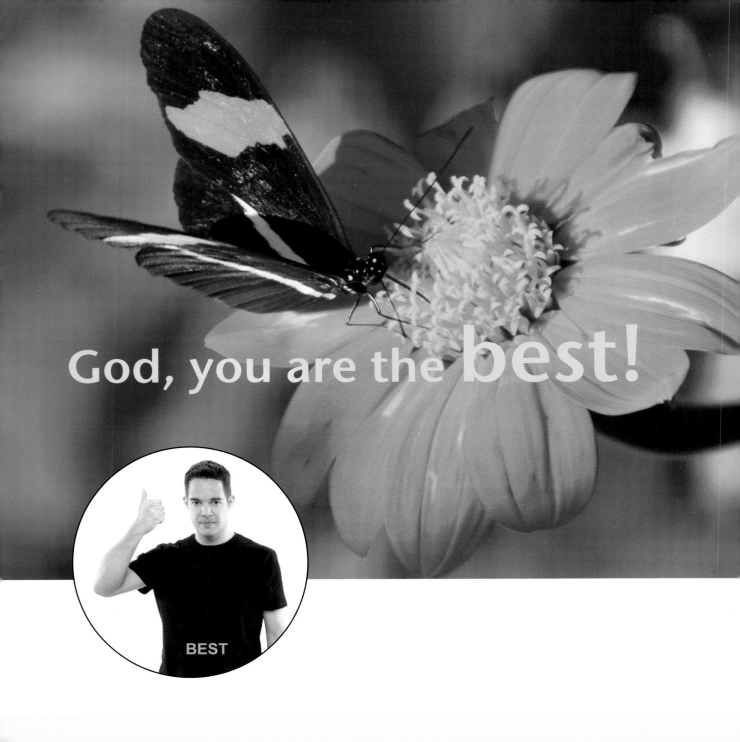

God, you are the best!

BEST

You create all things.
Your goodness and kindness are everywhere.
You are perfect.

You made me special!

God, you made me from head to toe.
I am your treasure!
You know everything about me.

MAKE

You always see me.

You have big plans for my life.

Thank you, God!

THANK YOU

You give me everything I need.
You love me.
You teach me.
You always help me.

I'm sorry, Jesus.

SORRY

Sometimes I make mistakes.
Sometimes I am unkind.
And sometimes I forget you are everywhere.
Still, you are my best friend and you forgive me.

Help me, Holy Spirit.

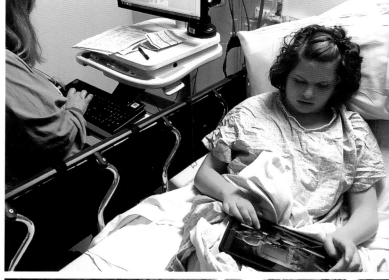

I need your Holy Spirit inside of me.
I want to grow and learn.
I want to make good choices.
I want to love others.
I want to be a giver.

When I feel weak or when I'm hurting,
you are always strong.

I'm listening to you.

LISTEN

I will slow down,
   wait,
      and watch for you.
         I don't want to miss anything you tell me.

Your Bible words are true.
You show me wonderful and beautiful things.

I believe in you!

You always keep your promises.
You are the most powerful, now and forever.

BELIEVE

LOVE

Heavenly Father, I'm sure glad we have
these special times together!
Let's talk again very soon.

I love you, Lord!
Amen.

Bible-based answers if your reader asks questions

Why does this book talk about Jesus, God, and the Holy Spirit?

It is fun and helpful learning to relate to God in His three important forms. Consider this: You are known to people in different ways like friend, neighbor, student, daughter or son, sister or brother, child or adult. Well, God makes himself known to us in some mysterious but wonderful ways too! Father God is the One who created each one of us. So He knows us better and loves us more than anyone. God also showed himself to us in the form of a man, His Son whose name is Jesus. Even though Jesus died one day a long time ago, He came back to life three days later and defeated death forever. Jesus still lives today as an invisible but most powerful Spirit. This Holy Spirit fills our hearts and minds with himself if we trust Him to forgive us and invite Him to lead our lives. It is an amazing, lifelong adventure to discover friendship with God in the three ways that He shows himself to us.

> Christ is the visible image of the invisible God. He existed before anything was created and is supreme over all creation, for through him God created everything in the heavenly realms and on earth. He made the things we can see and the things we can't see—such as thrones, kingdoms, rulers, and authorities in the unseen world. Everything was created through him and for him. He existed before anything else, and he holds all creation together.
> — Colossians 1:15-17

> And we know that the Son of God has come, and he has given us understanding so that we can know the true God. And now we live in fellowship with the true God because we live in fellowship with his Son, Jesus Christ. He is the only true God, and he is eternal life. — 1 John 5:20

> The Spirit of God, who raised Jesus from the dead, lives in you. And just as God raised Christ Jesus from the dead, he will give life to your mortal bodies by this same Spirit living within you. — Romans 8:11

Why is friendship with Jesus the most important gift we can ever receive?

Your friendship with Jesus is God's greatest joy! It also fills your life with all the best things on earth—joy, peace, and hope. With these priceless treasures, life is so wonderful that we can't fully describe it. Receiving Jesus' free gifts of friendship and forgiveness also means you will spend forever with God in the most beautiful and perfect place of all—heaven.

> But to all who believed him and accepted him, he gave the right to become children of God. They are reborn—not with a physical birth resulting from human passion or plan, but a birth that comes from God. — John 1:12-13

> God has given us eternal life and this life is in his Son. Whoever has the Son has life; whoever does not have God's Son does not have life. — 1 John 5:11-12

> You will show me the way of life, granting me the joy of your presence and the pleasures of living with you forever.
> — Psalms 16:11

How do we know God hears us?

God created us and knows everything about us. He promises to listen to His children and never leave us by ourselves.

O Lord, you have examined my heart and know everything about me. — Psalms 139:1

And we are confident that he hears us whenever we ask for anything that pleases him. — 1 John 5:14

We know that God doesn't listen to sinners, but he is ready to hear those who worship him and do his will. — John 9:31

Come close to God, and God will come close to you. — James 4:8

Why do some people have disabilities?

God is very creative! He loves everything He creates and He never makes mistakes. The way God sees it, the weaker things are often the most important. Sometimes we don't understand His reasons for being so creative about how He made each of us. But God's plans are always perfect.

Thank you for making me so wonderfully complex! Your workmanship is marvelous—how well I know it. — Psalms 139:14

Then the Lord asked Moses, "Who makes a person's mouth? Who decides whether people speak or do not speak, hear or do not hear, see or do not see? Is it not I, the Lord?" — Exodus 4:11

Jesus answered. "This [man was born blind] so the power of God could be seen in him." — John 9:3

The human body has many parts, but the many parts make up one whole body. So it is with the body of Christ. In fact, some parts of the body that seem weakest and least important are actually the most necessary. — 1 Corinthians 12:12, 22

The Lord always keeps his promises; he is gracious in all he does. — Psalms 145:13

The Lord doesn't see things the way you see them. People judge by outward appearance, but the Lord looks at the heart. — 1 Samuel 16:7

For our present troubles are small and won't last very long. Yet they produce for us a glory that vastly outweighs them and will last forever! — 2 Corinthians 4:17

We now have this light shining in our hearts, but we ourselves are like fragile clay jars containing this great treasure. This makes it clear that our great power is from God, not from ourselves. — 2 Corinthians 4:7

from the writer

One of my favorite places to meet with Jesus is outside on my deck, which overlooks peaceful trees and wetlands. My husband, Larry, and I have three grown daughters. Carly, our youngest, has Angelman Syndrome and lives at home with us. Carly isn't talking yet so I had the idea to write this book when we were teaching her how to pray.

I serve with Walk Right In Ministries and the Minnesota Disability Ministry Connection helping people connect in their communities and grow in faith, especially when they are facing challenges.

I would love to hear how your friendship with Jesus is growing and more about your own faith stories. You can write to me at lisa@walkrightin.org. My website is lisajamieson.org.

Lisa Jamieson

from the photographer

I've been leading and facilitating short-term missions for over thirty years, mainly in Belize and northern Italy. I graduated from Bethany College of Missions (now Bethany Global University) with an emphasis on missions and theology. My passion lies in the arts, serving as a musician, worship leader, voice teacher, and international photographer. I work full time with Adventive Cross Cultural Initiatives (ACCI), a Christian missions agency. As U.S. director, I focus on partnership development and member care, assisting missionaries who are serving in various countries around the world while also training team leaders for short-term missions. My husband, Luke, and I live near Minneapolis, MN.

I can be contacted at annlhinrichs@gmail.com. My website is annhinrichsblog.com.

Ann Hinrichs

Walk Right In Ministries helps people grow and connect with Jesus, their community and resources, especially when they are experiencing challenges like chronic illness, disability or caregiving for any generation.

The Minnesota Disability Ministry Connection is a non-denominational network of churches and like-minded organizations helping people of all abilities and their families encounter Christ and experience active belonging in the Church.

God is our merciful Father and the source of all comfort. He comforts us in all our troubles so that we can comfort others.
— 2 Corinthians 1:3-4

www.WalkRightIn.org

Walk Right In Ministries
PO Box 1932
Minneapolis, MN 55311

ACCI is a missions organization supporting a wide variety of ministry projects in locations all around the world. We partner with servant leaders who have passion and vision for a specific calling to a cross cultural ministry idea with the skills and gifts to match. Our purpose is to attract, equip, send, and serve the vision of passionate, effective leaders and teams who are focused on cross-culturally advancing the kingdom of Christ throughout the world.

We don't go around preaching about ourselves. We preach that Jesus Christ is Lord, and we ourselves as your servants for Jesus' sake.
— 2 Corinthians 4:5

www.adventive.ca

Adventive Cross Cultural Initiatives
239 Hampton Street
Rock Hill, SC 29730

Library of Congress Control Number: 2017918954
ISBN 978-0-9830333-4-9
First paperback edition 2018.
Printed in USA.

All inquiries should be addressed to:
Walk Right In Ministries, PO Box 1932, Minneapolis, MN 55311
www.WalkRightIn.org